The Wizard of Positive Living:

Tools to Improve Your Life

Clive Crossingham

The Wizard of Positive Living:

Tools to Improve Your Life

by CLIVE CROSSINGHAM

Published by Mental Image Publishing

ISBN 978-0-9572236-0-8

First Edition May, 2012

Printed in the United Kingdom

Contents

Dedication v

Introduction 1

Acknowledgements 5

Warning.. 7

About the Author.. 9

The Metaphor Explained 17

Positive Living 23

What Are You Waiting For? 25

Mastering Your Thoughts and Emotions...... 27

New Beginnings 55

Conclusion 89

Useful Contacts and Websites (UK) 90

Further Reading and Resources 91

Dedication

To my father, Joe Crossingham

1929–2011

It was beautiful while it lasted, the journey of my life,

I have no regrets whatsoever, save the pain I leave behind.

When you live in the hearts of the ones you love,

you surely never die.

(Well, until they die that is.)

Introduction

You already have the power

If you think about it, the story of *The Wizard of Oz* is a good metaphor for the journey of life.

Like Dorothy, if we want to grow and get the most out of life, we have to overcome our fears and self-limiting beliefs. We have to get all of our components (thoughts, feelings and actions) working together as a team, set goals, make plans, and take purposeful action with a clear direction in mind. It's also important that we enjoy the journey. That is the essence of positive living.

Whatever your individual journey goals are, *The Wizard of Positive Living* is a simple guide and a practical toolkit that can help you to improve your life and achieve greater happiness and fulfilment.

This book brings together ideas and techniques from the Positive Thoughts programme (Liverpool University), Cognitive Behavioural Therapy (CBT), Neuro-Linguistic Programming (NLP), and life coaching. It also owes much to the inspiring work of authors and motivational speakers like Paul McGee (the *SUMO* guy), Martin Davies (CBT trainer and cartoonist), Sue Stone (life coach) and Brian Tracy (business/life coach).

I met Paul McGee at one of his marvellous motivational seminars, where he demonstrated some of the ideas and techniques from his best-selling self-help book, *SUMO (Shut Up, Move On): The Straight-Talking Guide to Creating and Enjoying a Brilliant Life.* Paul and his wife were kind enough to accept my invitation to my first comedy gig at The Lounge bar in Warrington. Paul's seminar inspired me to want to become a successful author and life coach.

Martin Davies is an excellent CBT trainer and cartoonist. I learned a great deal from him at one of his entertaining CBT skills workshops. Martin's books, *SOD IT* and *SOD IT ALL! How to Deal With the Stress Virus in Your Life,* are full of his hilarious cartoons that put a light-hearted slant on the serious subjects of stress and depression. Martin's workshop inspired me to undertake further CBT training with the BSY distance learning college (BSY) to learn how to help people recover from common forms of mental distress.

I read Sue Stone's book, *Love Life, Live Life: How to Have Success and Happiness Beyond Your Wildest Expectations,* and met with her for a life coaching session as I was about halfway through writing this book. Sue helped me to define my goals and inspired me to acquire training as a life coach with the BSY and National Coaching Academy (NCA). During my NCA coaching skills training, I was introduced to the excellent works of coaching guru Brian Tracy. I strongly recommend Brian's books, DVDs, and seminars to anyone interested in learning about coaching.

All you need is within

You don't need any special skills or abilities to use the ideas and techniques contained in this book because (like the characters in 1939 movie, *The Wizard of Oz*) you already have all of the inner qualities that you need. All you have to do is recognise them and use them purposefully to achieve a more positive outlook and approach to life.

As you work through this book you will also need a pen and some paper to complete some simple tasks designed to help you to clarify what it is that you want from your life, and to create an action plan to get it.

I can't believe it's not Buddha

Apologies to any Buddhists that may be reading this, but I can't resist a good play on words. (And some crap ones.)

You may be pleased to hear that my approach to positive living doesn't require the reader to believe in any New Age universal powers. You see, it's not really important whether or not you believe that it's some kind of invisible power, the hand of God, your dead grandmother, or the normal workings of the human brain that guide you on your journey. That's a matter of perception. What's important is that the ideas and techniques explained in this book work and can help you to get more enjoyment out of your life and achieve your important goals and ambitions.

Acknowledgements

This book is inspired by the fictional characters of *The Wizard of Oz* story, but it also draws upon aspects of my own personal experience. It's important, therefore, to note that, for legal reasons, any likeness to any person or persons, living or dead, is entirely intentional.

I would like to thank the Warrington Disability Partnership for helping me to get my life and career back on track and for all of the wonderful work that they do to enhance the lives and promote the rights of people with disabilities and mental ill-health.

I would also like to thank my friends and mentors Sharon Eardley, Jan Hadfield, and the rest of the Positive Thoughts crew for putting up with me and helping to guide me on my journey.

Special thanks must go to Barbara Ardinger for correcting my spelling, grammar, and sentence structure, and for generally helping me to make this book gooder. You can learn more about Barbara and her work at her website www. barbaraardinger.com.

Tin Man x

P.S. I would particularly like to thank anyone that has ever intentionally caused me pain, as all of them, together with the other misfortunes that I have overcome in the journey of my life, have taught me something valuable about myself and humankind and helped me to grow and become a stronger person.

Warning

The ideas and techniques set forth in this book have the power to change people's lives and may result in new relationships, business start-ups, career changes, active retirement, voluntary work, dream holidays, extreme sports, and/or the purchase of dangerously overpowered motorcycles, sports cars, and speed boats. If you experience any of these symptoms or notice a general increase in fun, happiness, and fulfilment in your life, then you may be experiencing positive living.

About the Author

You can't polish a dog turd, but you can roll it in glitter.

- BA Hons social work
- Diploma in social work
- Chartered MCIPD
- CBT and NLP life coach
- Crisis intervention counsellor
- Positive thoughts trainer
- Mind mechanic
- Comedian

If (like me) you hate it when authors waffle on about themselves, you'll be relieved to hear that I have kept this chapter intentionally brief.

As a young man, I left school without any qualifications and experienced a somewhat 'unsettled' adolescence. I turned this around as an adult, however, by graduating from university and qualifying as both a social worker and human resources professional.

I grew up in a tough part of inner London and frequently changed schools, as we moved house due to my father's job. He was a policeman. Often the new boy in school, I was made to sit at the back of the class, where I was expected to try and catch up without much help. As a result, I soon fell out of love with school and truanted often. As an angry adolescent, I left secondary school without any qualifications and with a huge chip on my shoulder. I worked in a series of unfulfilling jobs in the building and catering industries, punctuated by periods of unemployment. I drifted into drug taking and graduated towards crime. I blamed my parents and society for my unhappy life, but in reality I lacked the maturity and skills to resolve my problems more constructively.

Things came to a head when I was sentenced to a custodial sentence for robbery. High on amphetamines, and low on self-esteem, I had robbed a bank.

Prison is a brutal place. I had to grow up fast to survive. On my release, I vowed never to return and moved away from London to seek a new life. Like Dorothy in the story of *The Wizard of Oz*, I set out in a new direction. In prison, I had somehow developed a brain, the courage to face up to my problems, and a strong desire to change my ways and to help others. My experience in prison had made me want to become a probation officer, but I was held back by my previous record, lack of qualifications, and the subtle and not so subtle discriminatory attitudes of some of the employers that I encountered. I finally got a break, however, when I was accepted to an access course for social workers in Manchester.

My experience of working as a social worker and manager of social care services now encompasses some twenty years, during which time I have worked with people with disabilities and mental ill-health in a broad spectrum of statutory, voluntary, and independent organisations across the north west of England.

In the early days, I did a lot of voluntary work for organisations like the Citizens Advice Bureau, the YMCA, and the Cheshire Probation Service. I gradually worked my way up via a number of part-time jobs including working as a community service supervisor and special educational needs officer. It was then that I began to learn sign language.

After qualifying, I worked for several years as a social worker and team manager in services for people who are deaf. As my career in social care developed, I went on to work as a senior manager, regulatory inspector, and free-lance management consultant. So far, I have enjoyed a largely rewarding and fulfilling career and been privileged to have met and worked alongside some truly inspiring and wonderful people (plus a thankfully small number of selfish and mean minded individuals).

In 2004, whilst working as a senior manager in a rapidly expanding private social care company in Liverpool and during a period of intense organisational restructuring, relationships became strained between me and some of my more ruthlessly ambitious colleagues. As a result I suffered a traumatic stress breakdown. Believing that I had been bullied and betrayed, I was diagnosed with Post Traumatic Stress Disorder (PTSD) and struggled with severe anxiety and depression for several years. During that difficult period I spent much of the day and night fixed to the sofa, unable to think straight or feel any emotions other than fear and a deep sense of sadness and despair. I experienced extreme sleep disturbance and developed a range of nervous tics that were made worse by my anti-depressant medication. I often felt so anxious that I was unable to leave the house, answer the phone, deal with correspondence, manage my affairs or do anything at all. My self-confidence and self-esteem had been replaced by fear and self-loathing. The only thing that gave me any sense of comfort was over-eating. (I'm not *fat*. It's just *emotional scar-tissue*.)

Nowadays, I'm 'out' about my personal experience of mental ill-health, but back then, not wanting to be tarred with the 'loony' brush (so to speak), I tried to deny the problem and put my symptoms down to some kind of physical ailment. I went to my doctor for blood tests, as I thought I might have a thyroid problem. I felt so tired and lethargic all of the time, it was as if I'd stumbled into a field of narcotic poppies like Dorothy and her friends.

Sadly, in our society mental ill-health still attracts a high degree of social stigma and discrimination and is often mistaken by the unenlightened - sufferers, their loved ones, employers, and onlookers alike as some kind of character flaw or weakness, which it isn't. Mental ill-health (or 'distress', if you prefer) is very common. As many as one in four of us may be affected by mental ill-health at some time in our lives.

This book is not intended to be a clinical study. Nor does it provide medical advice, but it does contain some helpful tips for mental well-being which should be everyone's concern.

Eventually, I received some help in the form of an effective talking therapy called Cognitive Behavioural Therapy (CBT). Thanks to this, and the support of the Warrington Disability Partnership (to whom I am eternally grateful), I was gradually able to rebuild my life and career and take my first steps on the road to recovery. CBT helped me to identify and change the dysfunctional thoughts and beliefs that were holding me back. My therapist helped me to gain insight to my condition and motivated me by helping me to set realistic and achievable goals for myself and to see them through. The Warrington Disability Partnership (WDP) is an enlightened organisation. Its workers are skilled and experienced in helping people with disabilities and mental ill-health to improve their lives. WDP's employment team helped me to find a pathway back into work. At first, my confidence and self-esteem were highly fragile, and I could only manage to work part-time. My memory and concentration were very poor. I constantly struggled with feelings of anxiety and had to resist a strong urge to run home where I felt safe. (There's no place like it.)

Whilst looking for paid employment, I was given a voluntary role developing policies and procedures for WDP. I hadn't been there long when someone walked into the office and asked if anyone knew how to drive a boat. It transpired that they needed someone to skipper WDP's fortuitously-named canal boat, *The Wizard*. I slowly raised my hand and said that I could do it. I had a small boat of my own and a qualification that enabled me to drive power boats.

Steering *The Wizard* along the historic Bridgwater Canal, through the beautiful Cheshire countryside, was a wonderful tonic for my spirits and self-confidence. I loved it so much that I carried on crewing *The Wizard* as a volunteer long after I got a full-time job. WDP and *The Wizard* have helped many people like me to rebuild their self-confidence and self-esteem. This wheelchair accessible canal boat is just one of WDP's wonderful services, and it brings joy to hundreds of disabled passengers and their families every year. I'm very proud to be associated with WDP and *The Wizard*.

It's true what they say: 'What doesn't kill you can make you stronger'.

Looking back at that difficult period in my life from a more positive perspective, I am now able to see that my ill-health, albeit a very painful experience, presented me with an opportunity for personal growth and a chance to re-focus my life. My experience of mental ill-health has taught me to pay closer attention to the content of my thoughts and beliefs and helped me to develop a broad range of valuable coping skills and strategies to manage stress and promote mental wellbeing.

In addition to helping me to learn about myself, this salutary experience has raised my awareness of the challenges faced by people living with mental ill-health and increased my general sensitivity to the suffering of others.

I have now returned to full-time employment and (as I wrote this book) work as a manager in social care services for older people, where I am also a trainer on my employer's employee support programme, Positive Thoughts for people recovering from common forms of mental distress.

CBT and Positive Thoughts have both had a positive impact on my outlook and approach to life and, in addition to equipping me with a broad range of effective ideas and techniques, have inspired me to find the courage and confidence to pursue my own goals and ambitions, including trying my hand at stand-up comedy, writing this book, training as a CBT therapist, getting involved with the 'Time to Change' anti-stigma campaign, and launching myself as a freelance life coach with the aim of helping others to positively enhance their lives. Please see my website at www. clivecrossingham.co.uk.

The inspiration for this book came to me during a Positive Thoughts session when I jokingly described myself as a 'Tin Man' because I was having difficulties connecting with my emotions ('dung, dung'). It was then that it occurred to me that the story of *The Wizard of Oz* is a good metaphor for the human journey of life and for talking therapies and self-empowerment in general.

In the best traditions of the 'hero journey', as described in the works of Joseph Campbell and others, having done battle with my personal demons, wicked witches, and flying monkeys, and reached a new understanding of myself and the world, I decided to write down the lessons that I have learned along the way in the hope that they may be of help and inspiration to others and help them to achieve greater happiness and fulfilment in their lives. Enjoy the journey.

'Fear can hold you prisoner. Hope can set you free.'

The Shawshank Redemption

The Metaphor Explained

On its surface, the story of *The Wonderful Wizard of Oz* by L. Frank Baum (published in 1900 and in 1939 made into the movie that we all know and love) seems to be little more than an entertaining children's fairy-tale. However, as a metaphor for our life's journey, the story becomes an interesting and engaging learning medium for people who want to develop their full potential and achieve a more positive approach to life. (Especially if you crow-bar it into a self-empowerment guide like this.)

In the story, Dorothy's life is turned upside-down by a tornado that crashes into her family's farm and transports her to a strange new world. In order to get home, Dorothy must follow the yellow brick road to reach the Emerald City to seek the help of the Wizard of Oz. At the start of her journey, she is encouraged and supported by the Good Witch of the North, who points Dorothy in the right direction and gives her a pair of magical slippers. Dorothy sets off down the yellow brick road leaving the safety of the land of the Munchkins far behind.

Along the way, Dorothy joins forces with a scarecrow, a tin man, and a lion, and together they resist the powerful Wicked Witch of the West and her winged monkeys and overcome the many obstacles placed in their path. To secure the help of the Wizard, the friends have to steal the witch's broom (the source of her power). Dorothy kills her using nothing more than a bucket of water.

When they eventually get an audience with the Wizard, the friends discover that he has no special magical powers. Instead, the Wizard tells the Scarecrow, the Tin Man, and the Cowardly Lion that they already had the inner qualities that they were asking for. The Scarecrow wanted a brain, the Tin Man, a heart, and the Cowardly Lion, courage. The Wizard explained that all they had to do was recognise their own abilities and use them purposefully.

Dorothy, whose greatest wish was to go home to Auntie Em and Uncle Frank in Kansas, also learns that she has had the means to get home all along. She can use the power of the magic slippers.

Life's Journey

We will take a look at the individual characters in a moment, but for now let's consider how the story can be used as a metaphor to describe each of us as we travel down the road of life, developing our potential and achieving our journey goals along the way.

In life, we sometimes make conscious choices and decisions about the directions that we wish to take and the goals that we wish to achieve. At other times (as in Dorothy's life), however, our decisions are shaped by events or adversity. We can choose to do nothing and stay in our comfort zone (as the Munchkins do), but if we want to develop and grow, we must overcome our fears and be clear in our minds about the direction we wish to take.

We need all of our components (thoughts, feelings, actions) to work together as a team to overcome the many obstacles in our path. We need to break the power of our self-limiting thoughts and beliefs, grow in self-confidence and self-esteem, and resist the negative influence of those who might seek to hold us back.

By making conscious decisions, using powerful practical measures, and taking purposeful actions, we achieve greater freedom and control over our lives and experience an increased sense of happiness and fulfilment. We may receive guidance and support from others along the way, but ultimately we realise our potential and achieve our goals ourselves. (Or something like that.)

Introducing the Characters

The story of *The Wizard of Oz* has been the inspiration for a host of artistic works including novels, films, songs, musicals and stage shows. I don't purport to be an expert on the entire Oz canon, nor do I intend to continually refer to the metaphor throughout all the chapters of this book. That could become a bit tiresome, even for the keenest of Oz fans. If you are interested in learning more about the Oz mythology, you might like to read *The Annotated Wizard of Oz,* as it contains a lot of interesting information about L. Frank Baum and his works.

In my interpretation, the Oz story is a metaphor for our life's journey in which the characters represent the key components of the human condition:

- Dorothy – symbolises the desire we each have to achieve our goals and potential.
- The Scarecrow – symbolises the brain or intellect (our thoughts and beliefs).
- The Tin Man – symbolises matters of the heart (our feelings and emotions).
- The Cowardly Lion – symbolises our body and actions. In the story, the lion wants courage. I believe that courage is best measured by a person's actions or inactions. Besides which, for my metaphor to work, I need one of the main characters to represent our body and actions and the Lion is the closest fit. (I think I got away with that one.)

- The Tornado – symbolises the tragedies and hardships of our lives.
- The Wicked Witch and her Winged Monkeys - symbolise our imaginary fears and self-limiting beliefs.
- The Good Witch – the embodiment of joy and emotional generosity.
- The Wizard – the embodiment of optimistic, positive thinking. Now some of you might be thinking, 'Hold on. Wasn't the wizard a phony?' Yes, he was. But in the popular film version of the story, he was also the person that helped the characters to develop their self-beliefs and recognise their inner strengths and abilities, much like a therapist or life coach would. (Now, where did I put that crow-bar?)
- The Yellow Brick Road – our journey through life and path to our goals.
- Emerald City – our journey goals.
- The magic slippers – empowering ideas and beliefs.
- Bucket of water – simple practical tools to help us achieve our goals. Later in this book, I'll show you how a bucket can help you to magically transform *your* life.
- Munchkin Land – our comfort zone.
- Toto – a Cairn Terrier.

I like metaphors because they can enable us to see something familiar in a whole new light. In the same way, I hope that this book helps you to take a fresh look at yourself and your life and what you would like to achieve with it.

Positive Living

Happiness first. All else will follow.

For most of us, life is not always a bowl of cherries. Sooner or later, tragic events happen to us all and (if we allow them) the daily hardships and monotony of the passage of life can wear us down until we begin to lose the joy of living.

The good news is that it does not always have to be that way because (whether we realise it or not) we all have the power to change, take control, and achieve happier and more fulfilling lives. By applying the ideas and techniques explained in this book you can help yourself to:

- Achieve a positive outlook and approach to life.
- Come to terms with and master your self-limiting thoughts, beliefs, and emotions.
- Pay attention to your physical, psychological, and (if you like) spiritual well-being.
- Set realistic goals, make plans, and see them through.
- Grow as a person and develop your true potential.
- Experience greater happiness and fulfilment.

Whatever your particular journey goals are - more money, a better job, a loving relationship, health and well-being, travel or to learn new skills, your overall aim should always be to achieve greater happiness and fulfilment in your life. Otherwise, what's the point?

What Are You Waiting For?

We're here for a good time, not a long time.

If you're reading this book, then I guess you've already decided that there are certain aspects about yourself or your life that you would like to change or improve. But just in case you were thinking about putting it off for a while, there are a couple of things that I would like you to consider.

The Days of Your Life

Imagine that each day of the week represents a decade in your life. Most of us can expect to reach Saturday or Sunday, and if we are lucky we may get a bank holiday. What day of the week (your life) are you on right now?

Mon	Tues	Wed	Thur	Fri	Sat	Sun	Bank Holiday
1-10 years	11-20 years	21-30 years	31-40 years	41-50 years	51-60 years	61-70 years	71 + years

The point is that time soon passes, and if you want to

change or achieve something in your life, the best time to start is always NOW.

'If we wait until the moment when everything is ready we will never begin.'

Confucius

Welcome to Someday Isle

Imagine that you live on an island called Someday Isle. It's a comfortable and safe place to be, but when you gaze out over the ocean, you can't help wondering what lies over the horizon. Deep down, you yearn to take a journey into the unknown, but to do so would mean leaving the safety of Someday Isle and venturing into the flow that surrounds the island. The people around you think that you are mad to want to leave and do all they can to persuade you to stay.

You could listen to those around you who would discourage you from starting your journey and remain in the safety of your comfort zone. Or you could overcome your natural apprehension and head out into the excitement of the flow, where you will develop and grow as a person as you journey towards your destination. In the end, it comes down to a simple choice:

'Get busy living or get busy dying.'

The Shawshank Redemption

Mastering Your Thoughts and Emotions

Be careful with your thoughts and beliefs.

They are the blue-prints for your emotions and actions.

Apologies to any psychologists that may be reading this. My explanations are intentionally simplistic.

If you're like me, then you would probably prefer to launch straight in and get started on the practical aspects of improving your life (see New Beginnings). But in order to make sense and full use of the techniques described in this book, I recommend that you invest a little time familiarising yourself with some of the basic ideas and principles that underpin them. This chapter also includes some effective techniques that can help you to pay attention to the content of your thoughts and emotions and get them working *for* you rather than *against* you.

Of central concern to talking therapies like Cognitive Behavioural Therapy (CBT) is the close relationship between our thoughts, feelings, and actions. CBT therapists help people learn to recognise and challenge their dysfunctional or self-limiting thoughts and beliefs with the aim of achieving improvements in their emotional well-being and behaviour. Our thoughts, feelings, and actions are so closely linked that a positive change in any one area can lead to positive changes in the other two.

One of the basic concepts of self-empowerment approaches like Neuro-Linguistic Programming (NLP) is that our minds have been programmed by our life experiences (both good and bad), which makes it possible for us to use certain techniques and strategies to positively reprogram or re-focus our minds (the unconscious mind in particular) to achieve beneficial outcomes.

'Whatsoever a man soweth, that shall he also reap.'

Galatians, 6:7

A common theme in self-empowerment approaches is the idea that in many ways we are all responsible for creating our own reality, i.e., we get the life that we choose.

If we think negative thoughts about ourselves and the world and focus on the negative aspects of our life, then we are more likely to achieve negative outcomes. Conversely, if we focus our minds on the positive aspects of life and concentrate our efforts on achieving positive goals, then we are far more likely to succeed and lead happier and more fulfilling lives.

In her book *Love Life, Live Life: How to Have Success and Happiness Beyond Your Wildest Expectations* (Piatkus Books, 2010), Sue Stone uses a lovely farming metaphor that helps to explain this concept. If we imagine that our conscious mind is the farmer, our unconscious mind the soil, and our thoughts the seeds, then we have to make a conscious decision about the crop that we wish to grow. If we sow bad seeds (negative/pessimistic thoughts), then we will reap a poor crop. If we sow good seeds (positive/optimistic thoughts), then we will experience a bountiful harvest, i.e., a happy and fulfilling life. As it is with farming, so it is with the mind. We reap what we sow.

When life gives you lemons, make lemonade.

An important aspect of positive living is the ability to adopt a positive mental attitude to life by looking for the positives in every situation and regarding our mistakes, failures and misfortunes as nothing more than opportunities to learn and grow. The mind of the average person processes thousands of thoughts per day. Many of these thoughts are typically about mundane issues relating to our daily existence food, warmth, shelter, etc., and others are about more interesting and creative matters. I like to refer to all of this mental activity as mind-chatter.

In his book *SUMO (Shut Up, Move On): The Straight-*

Talking Guide to Creating and Enjoying a Brilliant Life (Capstone, 2006), Paul McGee suggests that when you come to try something new or challenging, you may hear one of two voices chatting in your mind, either (1) your inner coach, or (2) your inner critic. (If you can hear several voices, other than your own, go see your doctor.)

Your inner coach will focus on your strengths and abilities, remind you of your past achievements, and tell you that you will succeed. This will make you feel happy, confident, and optimistic. Most importantly, you will try new things.

Your inner critic, on the other hand, will focus on your weaknesses, remind you of your past failures and shortcomings, and tell you that you will fail. You will feel unhappy, fearful, and pessimistic. Sadly, you are unlikely to even try to do something new or challenging, or if you do, you will be easily discouraged and soon give up.

In order to get the most out of life and achieve your goals, you have to take control of your mind chatter and make a conscious decision as to which voice you listen to - your inner coach or your inner critic. As always, the choice is yours.

In a typical day, the contents of our thoughts are likely to be a combination of both positive and negative thoughts, and for much of the time we may not be fully aware of the positive or negative undercurrent of our mind-chatter.

In order to develop a more positive outlook on life, it is important that you begin paying attention to the content of your thoughts and replace or reframe your negative, self-limiting thoughts with more positive and helpful ones. If you catch yourself thinking a negative thought, try using some of the following techniques. See which ones work best for you.

- Distract yourself. Do something that gives you pleasure or takes your mind off the negative thought.
- Say 'Stop!' Tell yourself to stop and refocus on something more constructive.
- Write it down. This helps to show negative thoughts for what they really are.
- Talk to a friend. Talk with someone that can help you to think more positively.
- Take action. Take some positive action to resolve the problem/concern.

I use a combination of these techniques. If I catch myself thinking a negative thought, I like to stop and replace it with a positive thought or reframe it using more positive terms. Doing something pleasurable, rewarding myself, or listening to my favourite uplifting music, helps too. If the thought relates to a real problem or concern, facing up to and resolving it is usually the best course of action. I find that having a sense of purpose, reminding myself of my desired goals, and taking some action toward achieving them is a particularly effective method for keeping myself positive and focussed on the good things in life.

Here's a tip. Try wearing a rubber band around your wrist. If you catch yourself thinking a negative thought, 'ping' it sharply and say aloud to yourself, 'Stop' (I mean stop thinking the negative thought, not stop pinging the elastic band…erm, stop that, too.)

Some negative thoughts are triggered so quickly and frequently they can be referred to as automatic thoughts. If you tell yourself often enough that you cannot do something, you will start to believe it and not even try. Next time you go to try something new or challenging, if your automatic thought is 'I can't', try reframing it by saying 'I can' or 'I can try', and then *just do it*. Taking purposeful action is a particularly important aspect of developing a positive 'can-do' mental attitude.

Changing your underlying negative or self-limiting beliefs may be a little trickier, as they are often very powerful, deeply rooted, and more difficult to spot. However, it is important to remember that your self-limiting beliefs are not real. Self-limiting beliefs are, basically, thoughts and emotions that have burrowed so deep in your mind that you no longer question them. With a little self-awareness and some practice, however, you'll find that it's possible to

THE WIZARD OF POSITIVE LIVING

identify, dismantle, and replace them with more positive and empowering ones.

You may need a little help to begin with, perhaps from a trusted friend, life coach, or therapist (as appropriate), but once you acquire the ability to master your negative thoughts and beliefs, you will soon begin to see yourself and the world, with all of its many wonders and possibilities, in a whole new positive light.

It doesn't matter what other people think about you.

All that matters is what you think about yourself.

From early childhood and throughout our lives, we develop certain beliefs about ourselves and our place in the world. Very often, the contents of our beliefs arise from our previous negative experiences (tragic events, failures, shortcomings, etc.), and the attitudes or behaviour of others towards us (unloving or abusive parents, critical teachers, overbearing bosses, being bullied at school or work, social stigma, discrimination, etc.). Although this kind of social conditioning may seem very powerful, it is important to see it for what it really is. None of us are simply the sum of what other people think we are. Our future cannot be determined exclusively by our past. Your negative thoughts and self-image may arise from the past attitudes and behaviour of others towards you, but only YOU are responsible for maintaining them and only YOU can fix them. Blaming other people, society, or the world will not help you do this.

The tell-tale signs of a negative underlying belief may be revealed by recurring thoughts, feelings, behaviours, and the things that we say about ourselves (both inwardly and outwardly). Here are some of my favourites (taken from my Internet dating profile):

- 'I lack confidence'.
- 'I am not good enough'.
- 'I am unattractive'.
- 'I am stupid'.
- 'I don't deserve good things'.

It takes a conscious effort to change your self-limiting thoughts and beliefs, but it is entirely worth it because when you change your mind, you change your view of yourself and the world. The ideas and techniques explained in this book are designed to help you to do this by sowing the seeds of the crop that you wish to reap, watering, feeding and nurturing those seeds, dealing with the weeds and pests, and becoming your own best inner coach or farmer or something (oh, you know what I mean).

'It is not the things of this world that hurt us, but what we think about them.'

Epictetus

It can sometimes be difficult to make a clear distinction between thoughts and emotions because they broadly emanate from the same place. (Apologies to anyone that has ever bought an 'I heart NYC' bumper-sticker. They're anatomically incorrect.)

If your overall desire is to achieve greater happiness and fulfilment in your life, then it's important that you are able to understand and manage your emotions positively. Human emotions have evolved over millions of years and are important components of our survival, social, and decision making toolkits. As the sensation of pain informs us that there is something wrong with our body, so do our negative emotions help by telling us that there is something wrong with a particular situation or that our needs are not being met. Negative emotions tell you when something needs to change.

An important skill, therefore, is the ability to pay attention to and understand your emotions and those of the people around you. This is often referred to as 'emotional intelligence', though I think I may be a bit 'emotionally retarded' (hence the Tin Man nickname). When I encounter a problem, I have a tendency to try and skip past the emotional weeping and wailing, finger-pointing, and blaming stages and get straight on with resolving it (probably because both my parents were Cybermen from *Dr Who*). This may sometimes make me appear a little insensitive, but it can be a helpful quality when I'm dealing with a crisis. (It's both my gift and my curse.)

All humans share the same basic emotional needs, for example, to feel safe, accepted, respected, and loved, etc., as described in the works of Abraham Maslow and others. When something is wrong or our needs are not being met, we experience negative emotions like fear, anger, anxiety, frustration, resentment, sadness, depression, jealousy, boredom, loneliness, etc. The two most powerful of these are fear and anger, and it may be argued that they are at the root of all the other negative emotions.

Whilst not particularly pleasant to experience, negative emotions release potentially helpful chemicals into our bodies and send us important messages. It's important to pay attention to these messages if we are to understand what is going wrong and how to fix it.

If we ignore or suppress our negative emotions, we may begin to experience a high degree of unhealthy stress or sadness in our lives and I can assure you (from painful personal experience) that you do not want to wander too close to the edge of that emotional precipice. Unhealthy stress gives rise to fear (anxiety), which, if not dealt with or resolved, can lead to anger, resentment, depression, and a whole host of unpleasant physical reactions and conditions, including pain, rashes, sleep disturbance, poor memory, and concentration, to name but a few. (Have I told you I've got amnesia?)

Very often, people experiencing such conditions go on to compound their problems by self-medicating with dangerous substances like alcohol, caffeine, recreational drugs, or food. Or they may engage in self-harming behaviour and/or experience suicidal thoughts. I have experienced all of these and do not recommend them to you.

If you or someone you know is experiencing a high degree of unhealthy stress, anxiety, or depression, then you or they need to seek help. I recommend talking to someone about it and contacting your doctor or one of the many helpful charitable or voluntary organisations that are available (see 'Useful Contacts UK').

Denying or suppressing your emotions is not the same as mastering them. Mastery involves recognising, understanding, and dealing with your emotions in a healthy way.

Parents of teenage children may find this next concept a little difficult to accept, but the fact is, short of physical violence or abuse, etc., *no one can make you feel anything* (if you don't let them). OK, so I may have made that last statement a little simplistic for dramatic effect, but it does make a serious point. Whilst the source or object of your emotions may at times be another person, *they* are not in control of your emotions. *You are.* You are not a puppet. You are in control.

For any given situation, there may be any number of possible emotional reactions or responses. Mastery involves exercising greater choice and control over which emotional response you choose to apply to a particular situation or set of circumstances.

Martin Davies uses a great example of this in his CBT training courses. Imagine that it is late at night. You are in town waiting for a bus, and you are approached by a drunk, who is staggering along, with a can of beer in his hand and singing loudly. He comes up to you and says, 'Give us kiss, darling'. What would your reaction be? Anger, aggression, fear, disgust, pity, or laughter? If you asked ten different people that question, you would probably receive several different answers.

Your actual response, of course, would probably depend on the circumstances at the time, i.e., whether you're alone, male or female, a kick-boxer, etc. The point is that there is a range of responses that can be applied to any situation, and with self-awareness and practice you can develop greater control over how you respond to thorny situations.

I believe another good example is road-rage. Imagine that you are driving along, minding your own business, and you are suddenly cut off by a boy racer in a flashy sports car. You have to slam on your brakes and let him in to your lane to avoid an accident. How would you react? Some people might shout, swear, and use angry or abusive gestures (or worse), whilst others might just roll their eyes in silent condemnation and feel relieved that nothing bad actually happened. When this sort of thing happens to me, I like to smile and wave as if the other driver has just thanked me for letting him or her in and feel thankful that no one got hurt. (OK, I may sometimes mutter 'dick-head' or such like under my breath, but I always smile, and wave politely nonetheless.)

If I allowed myself to react angrily, it wouldn't change anything that happened and would make me feel bad for having lost control of my emotions. When I control or modify my response, I come out feeling calm and happy. It takes a little practice, but next time something like that happens to you, try it. Once you master it, you can apply this approach to other aspects of your life (with the possible exception of dealing with your teenage kids).

The aim of emotional mastery is not to become an emotionless robot (or a Tin Man), but to understand and control your emotions rather than let them control you. In your day-to-day life, if someone or something upsets you or makes you feel angry or afraid, try to take some time out to be alone to make sense of the emotions that you're feeling. Try to resolve the problem in your mind and return to a state of inner peace and happiness as quickly as possible. If you can't do it immediately, then promise yourself that you'll do it later when you next have an opportunity to be alone.

Think through the situation and try to understand why you felt that way. Were you feeling threatened? Did what happened remind you of something that happened to you in the past? Does it go back to your childhood? Did it trigger a negative thought or belief that you hold about yourself?

If someone makes a derogatory remark about you or your performance or behaviour, think through the situation and decide whether or not their comments have any merit. If not, and you think the person might have been lashing out due to their own inner problems or selfish motivations, then tell yourself this and (if you are able) forgive them or feel some sense of pity or compassion towards them.

If the person's comments or remarks have some merit, however, acknowledge it, but don't beat yourself up over it. People make mistakes. That's how we learn. Say to yourself, 'OK, I made a mistake', and fix the problem if you can. Learn from it and move on.

Admitting to yourself that you made a mistake immediately removes or reduces the mistake's power over you. Remember, positive people don't make 'mistakes'. They just experience 'learning opportunities'. (Right?)

Another tip: It's easier to deal with life's problems if you are in a calm and relaxed mood. Before contemplating a difficult situation, try closing your eyes and concentrating on your breathing. Take slow, deep, controlled breaths in and out. (Listening to whale-music and sitting in the lotus position are entirely optional.) Controlled breathing is a quick and effective method for calming your thoughts and emotions. Writing things down can also help you to make sense of a difficult situation and deal with strong emotions. Don't spend too long doing this or keep going over and over the same problem, however. Resolve it as quickly as possible and move on.

Participants in the Positive Thoughts programme are encouraged to keep a daily mood diary in which they record their feelings. Keeping notes can help you to monitor your emotions. By identifying the people, situations, or activities (triggers) that make you feel particularly; glad, mad, sad, or fearful, you can learn to understand what your emotions are trying to tell you. I am now able to do this naturally in my mind without the aid of a diary. Well, anyway, that's my excuse for not doing my Positive Thoughts homework.

When we learn to recognise the people and/or situations that make us feel good or bad, we can make a conscious effort to concentrate on doing the things that give us pleasure and spending more time with people that help to make us feel good and energised ('radiators') and less time with those that sap our energy and make us feel miserable ('drains'). It's also important to remember that we, too, have the capacity to be either a radiator or a drain for those around us. Who are the radiators and drains in your life?

If you are able to recognise in advance that there are certain situations or people that make you feel bad, then you may be able to anticipate this and do something about it, i.e., *take some control*. You may be able to do this by avoiding or changing the situation, by preparing yourself mentally by telling yourself that you will be OK, and rehearsing a different script or emotional response in your mind. For example, if I'm going to meet someone who makes me feel anxious (usually because they've been a bit abrasive or hostile towards me), I imagine that I'm going to see a good friend and tell myself I'm looking forward to seeing them. When I meet the person, I'm usually able to do so with a genuine smile on my face. It may or may not change how the person feels or behaves towards me, but the important thing is that *I feel a whole lot better about the situation and myself for not allowing it to make me feel bad.* (That's right, a tiny bit smug and superior.) Your imagination is a powerful tool. Use it to your advantage.

When a really big emotional problem e.g., a disaster, tragic accident, or the loss of a loved one hits us, as they surely do, it's again important that we are able to acknowledge and come to terms with the strong emotions that we may be feeling with the aim of returning to some form of normal functioning within a reasonable period of time. It's normal to feel sad when bad things happen, but at some point you must let go of the feeling and get on with your life. It can be very helpful to talk to someone about what happened and how you feel about it. It's important to recognise that you're going through a healing process. You have to allow yourself some time to grieve. Then you have to move on. Remember that, time is the greatest healer and laughter the best medicine. If not, try Prozac (just kidding).

If someone has caused you harm (depending on its severity), an important part of the self-healing process can be your ability to forgive them. This is not to say that it is OK for them to treat you badly. It's not. But forgiveness is powerful mental exercise that can help you deal with past hurts and move on, rather than carrying around the emotional burden of hate and resentment with you for the rest of your life.

Forgiveness is not about helping the person that has caused you harm. It's about helping *you*. If you cannot find it within you to forgive them, then allow yourself to regard them at least with some degree of sympathy or pity. Sometimes the best you can do is to reach a state of acceptance that what has happened has happened and there's nothing you can do about it. That's fine if it helps you to leave the past in the past and get on with enjoying your life. One of the techniques that people use to help them to deal with past hurts is to write a letter to the person that has hurt them. The idea is to tell the person how they made you feel and what the impact of their behaviour has been on you and your life. The aim is, having got things off your chest, to assign the negative emotions to the past and leave them there. Very often, people either symbolically (and safely) burn or bury the letter. Then they move on. If any of this has struck a chord with you, try writing such a letter. But don't send it. Remember, positive people live in the now, not in the past.

There are two groups of people I greatly admire. The first are people that have discovered their passions in life and are actively pursuing them. The second are those that have been able to overcome adversity and turn negative situations into positive ones. Examples are the families of Stephen Lawrence and Suzy Lamplugh. In 1993, Stephen Lawrence was murdered whilst waiting for a bus in a highly publicised racist attack. The Lawrence family's tireless campaigning has had a significant impact on British legislation and the way that the police address racism. In 1986, estate agent Suzy Lamplugh disappeared when she went to meet an unknown client. So far, her body has not been found. Following her disappearance, Suzy's family set up a charitable organisation entirely dedicated to raising awareness of personal safety and addressing the causes of violence and aggression in society.

I'm referring to people that, following such a personal tragedy, have turned things around by doing something to help others, like setting up charitable trusts or support groups, campaigning for social change, or doing some voluntary work. For some people, this work can be an important part of the healing process and (in my opinion) is a wonderful and distinctly human trait.

Courage is not merely the absence of fear.

Of all the emotions that can have a negative impact on our ability to enjoy life and achieve our goals, fear (in all its guises) can be the most powerful and yet the most subtle. Fear and anger are essential components of our natural survival toolkit. Fear tells us when something is wrong. If we are in immediate danger, fear and anger instantly help us to decide whether to run or stand and fight. Well, that's great if you're facing an angry grizzly bear, because that's exactly the kind of situation that this 'fight or flight' mechanism was designed for. But the system is not perfect. It often makes mistakes. In our modern lives, our minds may perceive situations as threatening when they're not or exaggerate the degree of threat posed by relatively harmless stimuli.

Phobias are obvious examples of how this system can go wrong. People that experience phobias genuinely believe that they will come to some great harm if they come into contact with, or are in close proximity to, specific objects or situations that other people may take for granted. These can include cats, dogs, spiders, mice, snakes, or crowded or enclosed spaces. Other examples of how this system can go wrong include panic attacks and anxiety disorders, both of which can be highly distressing and debilitating for the people that experience them. The ideas and techniques in this book are designed to help anyone that wants to enhance or improve their life, but whilst they can certainly help to promote recovery from common forms of mental ill-health, such conditions usually require more specific interventions and may be beyond the scope of self-help alone. If you or someone you know is experiencing phobias, panic attacks, or excessive and persistent anxiety, then you or they should seek professional help.

What would you do if you were not afraid? Well, do that.

Fear may take many forms, but the particular fears that I want to focus on are the powerful self-limiting varieties that are able to construct seemingly insurmountable but imaginary barriers in our minds and prevent us from trying something new or challenging or pursuing our passions and goals in life.

Before we go much further, I would like to make a distinction between 'fears' and 'concerns'. Fears are often irrational or exaggerated and can prevent us from taking action. Concerns tend to be rational and related to the practical matters that require our attention in order for us to get on with our daily lives and carry out our jobs. In order to overcome a self-limiting fear, we must first identify, understand, and face up to that fear. In my experience, there are broadly three (related) fears that tend to hold people back: (1) the fear of the unknown, (2) the fear of failure, and (3) the fear of rejection. There are a number of simple measures that we can use to disarm and overpower each of those fears.

The first important thing to remember is that fear (like the Wicked Witch in the Oz story) only exists in our imagination and cannot actually cause us any bodily harm. So why be afraid?

'I would worry if I thought it helped.'

My mate Derek

Fear of the Unknown

Knowledge is your greatest ally against the fear of the unknown. As my skydiving instructor used to say, 'Knowledge dispels fear'. (He was saying this as he was demonstrating the correct way to lie on a stretcher if you're being lifted into an ambulance.) As it is with extreme sports, so it is with anything in life that takes us out of our comfort zone. At first we may feel naturally apprehensive or afraid, but as we acquire knowledge, our confidence grows and our fear and feelings of uncertainty diminish.

If you are thinking about trying something new or making a significant change in your life, then do some research. Learn as much as you can about the subject. If you find yourself dwelling on the things that might go wrong, write them down and use your imagination to come up with ideas for what you can do if things don't work out quite as well as you hope. Make a back-up plan (or carry a reserve parachute).

'Failure is only failure if you allow it to be.'

The Fear of Failure

Action is your greatest ally against the fear of failure. The fear of failure must be the most common reason people give for not taking risks, trying something new, or pursuing their ambitions in life. And yet, have you ever stopped and asked yourself what's so bad about failure? Trial and error is how we humans learn, and anyone who has never failed at something has never learned anything.

Yes, failure is a state of mind. It's a matter of perception. It can be changed. If you try something, fail, and give up, then you have surely failed. If, on the other hand, you try something, fail, learn from it, and try again, then you have learned a valuable lesson in life.

It seems that some people take setbacks to heart rather than to mind. Failure hits them hard in the self-esteem department. It feeds their negative, self-limiting beliefs (probably acquired in childhood) and returns them to a child-like emotional state. If you want to escape the monotony of your mundane life and follow your passions, you will have to venture out of your comfort zone at some point. Instead of seeing failure as the enemy and taking it to heart, try *embracing fear* as a friend and teacher. If your fear of failure is holding you back, consider this: rather than focussing on the possible cost of failure, consider the possible cost of missed opportunities. Remember, nobody's perfect, and one person's failure is another person's lesson or opportunity for personal growth. Failure is a matter of perception.

Here's a useful tip. If you decide to take a risk and pursue your dreams, then try asking yourself these two important questions. First, what's the worst thing that can happen? Second, how long would it take you to recover? In all probability, if things don't work out as well as you hoped, you won't suffer any physical harm, but you will learn and grow as a person, you will recover quickly, and very often, even if you don't reach your desired destination, by taking purposeful action, you will achieve some equally interesting and satisfying outcomes. It took me five years, and several attempts, for example, to get into university. I wanted to be a probation officer, but instead I ended up as a dually qualified social worker and human resources professional.

The Fear of Rejection

Rejection is a natural part of life and should not be feared. When looking for a new job, we tend to accept the competitive nature of the process, and when we experience rejections, we tell ourselves, 'That's just the way it goes, better luck next time, there's a better job just around the corner, there's plenty more jobs in the sea'.

Rejection in relationships can be a little tougher, but if you consider the divorce rate, for example, it's really just as much a normal part of life as being rejected for a job. It may not feel like it at the time, but rejection is *not* the end of the world. In the great scheme of things, it's nothing to be feared. If rejection happens to you, it may sting for a bit, but *you will recover*. Remember to look for the positives in every situation. Know that positive people see rejection as an opportunity to make a fresh start or new beginning.

For some people, the fear of rejection can become a self-limiting way of thinking that holds them back and prevents them from reaching out for the things they want in life. Dating is a good example of this. If there is someone you like, and you would like to ask them out on a date, but you don't because of your fear of rejection, then you're giving yourself no chance with that person, or them with you. You end up creating a self-fulfilling prophecy. 'He/she will never go out with me, so I won't ask them'. (And so the prophecy becomes true.)

Imagine for a moment that you are lying on your deathbed with your family and friends standing beside you. Looking back on your life, what do you regret more? The things that you've done or the things you haven't done? (OK, in my case, it would have be a little from column A and also a little from column B.) The point is, don't let your fear of rejection hold you back. Rejection cannot cause you any physical harm. Like everything else in life, if it happens to you, accept it, feel the sting for a short time, then move on and seek out new opportunities or beginnings.

Mastering your thoughts and emotions is an important aspect of achieving happiness and fulfilment. Another is the ability to share your emotional generosity with others. Emotional generosity is about helping others to feel positive and good about themselves. Emotionally generous people smile a lot, give praise and encouragement, show love and affection, and help and support others without expecting anything in return. A little tip for parents here - you cannot spoil a child with love and affection.

In the next chapter, I will describe two techniques we will be using to help us to achieve our goals, visualisations and affirmations. Visualisations and affirmations can help us as we use our senses and imagination to consciously reprogram our unconscious mind by sowing, feeding, and watering the seeds of the crop we wish to reap.

When we set clear goals for ourselves, we set another powerful part of our mind called the reticular activating system (or the 'rotating sprinkler system', as a good friend of mine likes to call it) into motion. Before I learned the correct term for this system, I used to call it the Morris Minor syndrome. One of my first cars was a Morris Minor, and before I owned one, I hardly ever noticed their existence. As soon as I decided I wanted to buy one, however, I began noticing Morris Minors everywhere. Our reticular activating system helps us by focussing our attention on the things that are meaningful or important to us. If you're clear in your mind about the goals you want to achieve, your reticular activating system will help you to seek out the relevant people, resources, and opportunities you need to make progress and succeed.

It's a bit like giving your mind a shopping list. For example, when I decided to start out as a life coach, I realised that I knew very little about marketing. But as soon as I set learning about marketing as a goal for myself, I began noticing how other people market their services. I also began noticing advertisements for printing services, website designers, and other services, even when I wasn't particularly looking for them. Within a few days I received an e-mail containing an advertisement for a marketing training course. I promptly booked myself a place on it. I had consciously gone looking for some of the things that I needed, but many others just seemed to pop up. That's because both the conscious and unconscious parts of my mind had a clear understanding of my goals and were busy working together to help me find the resources and opportunities I needed.

In the next chapter, I will show you how to consciously access this powerful system and create your own personal action plan with some clear priorities, goals, and actions for your conscious and unconscious mind to focus on.

New Beginnings

Imagine your perfect life. What would it be like?

This chapter is about the practical aspects of making the desired changes and improvements to your life and sets forth as a series of simple tasks (mostly lists) designed to help you to be clear in your mind about the things that are important to you and what you would like to achieve. The tasks are also available in the form of a workbook called 'My Action Plan' (MAP), which can be downloaded from my website, www. clivecrossingham.co.uk. But you can just write them down in a notebook or journal or on a sheet of paper. That works just fine.

Before deciding on how you would like your life to be in the future, let's take a few moments to look at your life as it is now.

Task 1. Make a list of your achievements to date.

MY ACHIEVEMENTS

Degree
Social work qualification
HR qualification
Teaching qualification
Positive Thoughts training
CBT training
NLP & Coaching training
Pilot's license
Glider pilot certificate
Advanced driver's licence
RYA Powerboat licence
Skydiving
Winner of comedy competition
Sense of humour
Caring & generous nature

Making a list of your achievements helps you to remind yourself of your many talents, skills, and abilities. You may want to develop your present achievements further or acquire some new skills, but whatever your goals are, it is important that you absolutely believe in your ability to achieve the things you set your mind to. You might also like to include on this first list some of the characteristics that you like about yourself to help boost your self-image and remind you of your many good qualities.

Helpful tip. When thinking about your past achievements, remind yourself of the good and positive feelings that you had when you achieved them. Close your eyes, take yourself back in time, and imagine yourself achieving the things you listed and feeling those good feelings again. Say out loud how you feel, e.g., 'I feel happy, confident, and proud', etc.

Task 2. Make a list of any obstacles that you have overcome in your life.

OBSTACLES

Moved schools a lot as a kid. Left school with no qualifications

Redeemed misspent youth

Difficulties getting into university. Kept trying

Survived mental illness

Overcame discrimination in employment market

Very often, when we think about making changes to our life or trying something new or challenging, the first thoughts that tend to pop into our minds are the reasons why we 'can't'. I like to think of this as an automatic 'can't do' attitude.

When you set out to achieve your desired goals, there may be a number of tasks you will need to perform and obstacles you will need to overcome. To do this, you need to develop and maintain an automatic 'can-do' attitude. By thinking about your past achievements and the barriers or adversities that you have already overcome in your life, you're reminding yourself of your inner strengths, your resilience. It's important for you to feel proud of your achievements and think of yourself as a strong and capable person…*because you are.*

Helpful tip. Remember, once they have made up their mind about what they want to achieve, positive people are only concerned with one question. *How to do it.*

Task 3. Make a list of all the things that you are grateful for in your life.

<u>MY GRATITUDE LIST</u>

Children

Grandson

My job/income

My health/wellbeing

My home & neighbourhood

My sense of humour

My cooking skills

Making a list of the things in your life that you're grateful for, and looking at it often, reminds you of the good things in your life. It also helps you maintain a positive mental attitude.

Helpful tip. Your list can include anything you like, e.g., your; family, friends, pets, health, home/garden, job, income, talents, skills, possessions, past experiences, memories, etc. Some people like to keep their lists by their bed, on their desk, on the door of the refrigerator, in their diary, or pinned to a notice board.

Task 4. Make a list of your passions and pleasures in life.

MY PASSIONS and PLEASURES

Spending time with family
Holidays/travel
Cooking/eating out
Gardening
Fishing
Gym
Cycling
Swimming
Snorkelling
Watching sports
Comedy
Music/concerts
Sparkling wine
Candlelit baths
Having sex
Films & documentaries
Driving
Motorcycles
Aircraft
Boats
Completing DIY projects
Teaching/training
Studying/writing
Equality, diversity, anti-stigma
Helping others

Much of our life is spent working and doing the mundane things we all have to do to just to get by. But it's essential for our general well-being to have some balance in our lives by making time to follow our passions and do the things that bring us pleasure. If we're very lucky, the work we do also reflects our passions in life and gives us a deep sense of purpose.

Do you live to work or work to live?

Your list of pleasurable activities is personal to you and will no doubt contain some varied and interesting pastimes. But how much time do you actually spend with the people that matter to you or doing the things that you are passionate about and make you feel happy and fulfilled?

'The best things in life really are free. Well some of them, anyway.'

A simple and effective way to increase your sense of happiness and fulfilment is to make a conscious effort to increase the number of pleasurable activities you take part in each week. (I know. That's a 'no-brainer'.) These do not have to be expensive or extravagant activities, indeed some of the best mood enhancing activities require little or no money. For example:

- Socialising. Spending time with family, friends, and neighbours. Connecting with your local community.

- Being active. Walking, cycling, swimming, dancing, gardening, playing ball with the kids, going to the gym, or taking a Zumba class.

- Connecting with nature and appreciating the world around you. Taking an interest in the changing of the seasons. Going for walks in the park, along the beach, or in the countryside. Visiting a nature reserve, getting involved with a conservation group, growing plants, flowers or vegetables. Walking the dog, feeding the birds, hugging a tree (sorry, couldn't resist).

- Learning and trying new things. Reading a new book, learning a new skill, trying a new recipe, researching an interesting subject, joining a class or taking a correspondence course.

- Treating and pampering yourself. Building a little play-time into your week and rewarding yourself with some treats, e.g., listening to your favourite music, relaxing in a hot bath, meeting up with friends for coffee, enjoying a glass of wine, buying some new clothes, having a make-over, planning a trip or a holiday, having sex. (I know that's twice I've mentioned it now. Freud would have a field day.)

- Giving to others. Doing something nice for a relative, friend, neighbour, or stranger. Getting involved in your local community, joining a campaign, giving to charity, doing some voluntary work.

- Making plans and seeing them through (discussed in detail below).

'Remember, it's often the simple things in life that give us the most pleasure.'

Task 5. Increase your pleasurable activities and rewards.

Make a conscious effort to fill your life with the things that bring you pleasure and treat or pamper yourself often. Start today. Take a look at your list of passions and pleasures and choose things that you can do today, this week, this month, this year, and add them to your schedule. Bring some pleasure into your life.

<u>MY SCHEDULE OF FUN</u>

Cook a new recipe – after work today

Phone an old school buddy – this evening

Relax in bath with candles – tonight

Take dog for a walk in the park – every day

Feed the birds – every day

Buy new CD and listen to it – this week

Invite friends over to watch the game on TV - Friday

Haircut & new clothes – Saturday

Meet friend in town for lunch - Saturday

Visit Mum and Dad – Sunday

DIY jobs – day off

Give blood – monthly

Give to charity – monthly

Plan a trip/holiday – summer

Planning activities and seeing them through is a particularly good mood-enhancing activity in itself, but it's also important to be spontaneous and adventurous by trying new things and seizing opportunities for fun as they arise. When was the last time you tried something new?

Helpful tip. Pick up a copy of your local newspaper or Google the Internet to see what's going on in your area. Try something new.

'Dream as if you'll live forever. Live as if you'll die today.'

James Dean

Task 6. Create a bucket-list.

<u>MY BUCKET LIST</u>

Travel; Australia, USA, Mexico, Ireland, Africa, Caribbean, India, Thailand, Canada...

Stay in a log cabin by a lake

Ride in a hot-air balloon

Try white water rafting

Try scuba-diving

Catch a marlin/sailfish/tarpon

Study CBT and NLP

Write a book

Become a successful life coach

Buy a new car and motorcycle

Join an anti-stigma campaign

Try stand-up comedy

Be on the first mission to Mars

If you're not familiar with the term 'bucket list', it's an expression made popular by a film of the same name in which the two main characters, played by Jack Nicholson and Morgan Freeman, are both terminally ill and meet in hospital. They decide on a plan to do all the things they've ever wanted to do before they 'kick the bucket' (die). This idea is also the inspiration behind the second series of the TV programme *An Idiot Abroad,* in which Ricky Gervaise and Stephen Merchant get their reluctant friend Karl Pilkington to take part in activities taken from other people's bucket lists with comic effect.

In the story of *The Wizard of Oz,* Dorothy kills the witch with a bucket of water. Who would imagine (apart from L. Frank Baum) that a bucket of water could contain such power? When I wrote my first bucket list, it had a tremendously powerful effect on me. It helped me to rediscover the joy of living. Until then, I had not realised how much I'd closed my mind to the wonderful experiences and possibilities that life has to offer. Not anymore. I don't know how much time I've got left, none of us do, but I'm determined to enjoy every moment as best I can.

Helping people to create their own bucket lists is one of my favourite exercises because it often (1) inspires people to come up with some fantastic ideas and (2) kick-starts them into taking action. I like to call these 'light-bulb' moments. You can create your list on your own, but it can be a lot of fun working with another person or doing it as a group exercise, e.g., at one of my workshops. See my website www. clivecrossingham.co.uk for more information on my workshops.

We spend so much of our lives engaged in boring or mundane activities that having a bucket list reminds us that there's much more to life. I once heard a lovely rationale for having a bucket list. It's like looking ahead (instead of back) at some of the highlights of your life.

> *'Your imagination is your preview of life's coming attractions.'*
>
> Albert Einstein

Start by making a list of about ten things that you would like to do, see, experience, or achieve before you die. While you can have as many goals on your list as you like (some people have over 100) ten is a good starting point. Be creative and add new goals to your list as they occur to you. Your goals don't all have to be big or ambitious, just anything that will bring happiness, fulfilment or purpose into your life.

People sometimes criticise this kind of 'no limits' creative thinking as being fanciful or unrealistic. Ignore them. When making your list, use your imagination and don't restrict your ideas just because they might seem unrealistic. (We will come back to the subject of being realistic in a little while.)

I used to think that being stuck in a rut was simply a matter of doing the same old boring things day in, day out, but I now realise that it's much more than that. It's also not being able to *imagine* your life being anything different. As children, we are capable of believing that anything is possible. We can imagine being anything we want to be. But as we grow up, all too often we seem to lose or suppress our ability to imagine that we can achieve a better life for ourselves and others.

Most people's bucket lists include a combination of both achievable and seemingly impossible goals and ambitions. I believe that the thinking that goes into creating a bucket list is just as important as the goals themselves. Going through the creative thought process can help to loosen the shackles of your imagination and get you into a more creative and optimistic frame of mind. It's also a lot of fun.

Helpful tip. Treat your bucket list as a living document (rather than a one-off exercise) and refer to it and amend it often.

Task 7. Think about your life as it is now and consider the following questions.

- What aspects of your life are working well?

- What aspects would you like to change?

- What aspects would you like to change the most?

There may be many things about yourself that you like and aspects of your life that are working well. It's good to remind yourself of these. But the main purpose of this task is to focus on the aspects of yourself or your life you would like to change or improve.

In my coaching sessions and workshops, I sometimes use a tool called the Wheel of Life to help people to identify and prioritise up to eight aspects of their lives they might like to change. The Wheel of Life, which is a visual representation of a person's priorities for change, is available as a free download from my website www.clivecrossingham.co.uk. A simple list works just as well.

CHANGES/IMPROVEMENTS

Better job/more money

Gaining a qualification

More travel/holidays

More socialising/fun

New car/motorcycle

Home improvements

Lose weight/get fit

More romance

Your list can include anything about yourself or your life you would like to change, e.g., relationships, work, money, education, training, health, fitness, diet, social life, appearance, personal characteristics, home, car, motorcycle, holidays, hobbies, interests, talents, skills, experiences etc., anything at all, so long as an improvement in that area will help you feel happier and enrich your life. At this stage, you may use some very general terms like 'new job, 'more travel', lose weight', etc., as we will be fine-tuning these into more detailed and specific goals and action plans in the coming sections.

You may have identified any number of things that you would like to change or improve about yourself or your life, some of which will be more important than others. It is important to set priorities for the changes we make, as experience shows that if we try to tackle too many things at once, we may feel overwhelmed, lose focus, and give up. A far more effective approach is to choose three high priority areas and focus our efforts on achieving them first. An easy way to do this is to rate the items on your list out of ten according to how important they are to you. Rate them 1 to 10, 10 being very important and 1 being relatively unimportant.

CHANGES/IMPROVEMENTS	
Better job/more money	10
Gaining a qualification	10
Lose weight/get fit	10
More travel/holidays	8
More socialising/fun	8
More romance	8
New motorcycle	6
Home improvements	6

As we can see from this list of priorities, getting a better job with more money, gaining a qualification, and losing weight and getting fit are of highest importance. There's nothing to say, of course, that this person cannot take action in relation to the other items. Indeed, some of the items might be a quick fix, e.g., planning a holiday, buying a motorcycle, joining an Internet dating site, completing some DIY jobs, etc., but I recommend that you concentrate most of your efforts on achieving your goals to which you've given the highest scores.

There are many methods you can use to rank or prioritise the items on your list. It doesn't really matter which one you use, so long as you identify a short list of about three aspects of your life or goals that you would most like to focus on.

Task 8. Decide what your most important goal is.

From your short list of important goals, choose your most important goal, i.e., the one goal that if you achieved it tomorrow would have the most positive impact on your life. This is the goal you should concentrate on and spend most of your time and energy trying to achieve.

In the next section, I will show you how to create a realistic and achievable personal action plan, and demonstrate how visualisations and affirmations can help you to positively reprogram your mind to focus on achieving your goals.

'Efforts and courage are not enough without purpose and direction.'

John F Kennedy

Goal Setting and Action Planning

Very few people have a clear plan for the important aspects of their life, and fewer people have a written plan. Having a written plan may not be terribly important, but planning most definitely is. Experience shows that if we write something down, we are far more likely to act. Remember, one of your aims is to positively reprogram your mind to focus on achieving your desired goals. Writing goals in a particular way (as shown below) is one method of doing this.

'Begin with the end in mind.'

Steven Covey

Most people seem to just drift along through their lives with no real sense of purpose or idea of what they are trying to accomplish. That's OK if you're happy living that way, but if you want to get more out of life, you must be clear in your mind about what you want and how you are going to get it.

By now, if you've been following the previous steps, you should have some idea about some of the things that you really want to do or achieve in your life. In this section, you will learn how to turn these broad ideas into a clear action plan with some specific, realistic, and achievable goals.

Whatever your goals are, you must absolutely believe that they are attainable. If you set realistic goals, think positively, and act purposefully, you will soon begin to see the results of your efforts and your self-belief and confidence will grow. Remember the magic words: *'I can!'*

*'Actions speak louder than words, but both
usually start with a thought.'*

Task 9. Define your goals.

Starting with the most important goal on your list, think a little deeper about the areas of your life that you would like to change or improve. Now turn each item into a clearly defined statement or goal that says exactly what you want to achieve and by when (see the table below). As you are writing, think about *why* you want to achieve each goal and what achieving it would mean to you. The more reasons you can give for achieving your goals, the more motivated and committed you will be to succeed.

Another handy tip. When writing goals, it is always better to write them in the present tense as if you have already achieved them and include some information about how that makes you feel. Reading your goals out loud to yourself or to a friend can also be beneficial and can help with the reprogramming process. At this stage, you may want to write your goals in pencil because it is likely that you will want to modify them as we progress (not a problem if you're using a computer). Here are three examples.

Goal 1. Getting a Better Job with More Money.

It is a year from now, and I'm a manager in my company. I'm enjoying the responsibility, earning 30 percent more pay, and can afford to buy more of the things that I want. I feel great job satisfaction. I'm excited about going to work each day.

Goal 2. Gaining a qualification.

It is three years from now, and I have graduated from college with a qualification in business management. I am now able to apply for more senior positions. I feel capable and confident in my knowledge and skills as a manager.

Goal 3. Losing weight and getting fit.

It is six months from now, and I am 14 pounds/6 kilograms lighter and eating a more healthy diet. I am going to the gym three times per week and swimming at the weekend. My clothes fit better, I have more energy and enthusiasm, and I look and feel great.

When writing your goals you can use whatever terms you like so long as they are clear and meaningful to you. A popular (and easy to remember) method uses the acronym SMART (Specific, Measurable, Achievable, Realistic, Time-bound) to remind you to make sure that your goals contain the important components. As you write your goals, be SMART and consider the following questions:

Specific. Are your goals clear and specific? The more detailed your goals are, the easier it is to see what actions you need to take to achieve them. This is true for all goals, no matter which aspect of your life you wish to improve - job, money, skills, health, fitness, new car, holidays, etc. Some people even apply the SMART program to their romantic relationships so they have a very clear idea about how they would like their ideal partner to look, sound, dress, and behave, etc. That's OK if you're drop-dead gorgeous or a stalker, but I prefer to be a bit more open-minded when it comes to people. Nevertheless, you may have a few non-negotiable items like caring nature, good sense of humour, non-smoker, etc.

For demonstration purposes, I have cheated a little with my examples because in reality each one subsumes a combination of goals that could easily be divided into separate and more specific goals or sub-goals (but you get the idea).

Measurable. Do your goals contain elements that can be measured? For example, a *30 percent increase* in pay/income, going to the gym *three times per week*. If they are measurable, then it's much easier to monitor your progress and recognise when you have met your goals.

Achievable. Are your goals within your ability to achieve them? Do you have all of the skills and resources you will need? If not, how will you get those skills and resources?

Realistic. Given your current situation, are your goals realistic, or do they need to be modified to bring them within your reach? For example, a 50 percent increase in pay may be a little ambitious to begin with. A 10 to 20 percent increase may be more realistic.

If my goal was to lose 14 pounds/6 kilograms in a week, this would probably be unrealistic (if not, I would have already done it and written a best-selling slimming guide). A timescale of six months or an approximate rate of two pounds or one kilogram per month is more achievable. If your goals seem a little unrealistic then they probably are, so think about what you might do to make them more achievable and within your reach.

Time-bound. It's important to set yourself a realistic timescale in which to achieve your goals, as this can help to measure your progress and motivate you to take action. Some timescales may not be entirely within your control, like the duration of a training course, but many others will be. Try not to set timescales that are too far into the future, as you may feel that you have plenty of time and procrastinate until the deadline is upon you.

Suppose you set a maximum timescale of one year. When you review your progress in a year's time, if you have not fully achieved your goal, then you can simply revise your timescale by moving it back six months or a year.

By now you should have your list of SMART goals, each one written in the present tense, and with a realistic timescale for when you are going to achieve each goal. The list will form the basis of your action plan (see below), but before we move on, I would like to formally introduce you to visualisations and affirmations.

If visualisations and affirmations are something new to you, the next task may seem a bit weird and New Agey at first, but stick with it. Imagining yourself achieving your goals can really help you to positively focus your mind and grow your self-belief. (Trust me, I'm a social worker. Well, trust me anyway.)

Task 10. Create helpful visualisations and affirmations.

Taking each of your goals, one at a time, use your imagination and travel forward in time to the date you have set as the target for when you will have achieved that goal. In your imagination, it is one year from now. You have achieved your goal. How does achieving your goal look, feel, and sound to you? Where are you and who are you with? How are you dressed? How is the weather? Imagine that you are there now. Smile and actually experience the good and positive emotions that you are feeling. Feels good, doesn't it?

Speak to yourself. Say something like this: *It is one year's time and I have achieved* [insert goal]. *The sun is shining, the sky is blue, the birds are singing in the trees. I am with my family and friends and they are all smiling and congratulating me on my success. I feel happy, confident, and full of the joys of life. What a beautiful day!*

Now develop a positive affirmation and repeat it to yourself often (either out loud or in your mind). Affirmations are short powerful statements that can be used to help positively reprogram your mind to focus on achieving your goals. Perhaps it could go something like this: *I am a strong and capable person. I can and will achieve my goals and whatever I set my mind to.*

If you say something often enough, your unconscious mind will believe what it hears. If you want to achieve a goal, you must absolutely believe that it is possible and that you are capable of achieving it.

If you have read 'Mastering Your Thoughts and Emotions' (page 27, above), you may recall the importance of sowing the seeds of the crop that you wish to reap. Visualisations and affirmations can help you to achieve this.

If you have difficulty visualising what achieving your goal looks like, don't worry. Just concentrate on how it *feels* to succeed. Some people use pictures and images from magazines or the Internet to make a visualisation board. Affirmations are usually personal, so use whatever words you like so long as they are meaningful and believable to you.

Now let's turn your goals into a personal action plan that will help you to answer that most important question of all: *How are you going to achieve your goals?* I can guide you, but only you can find the answer to that question because you are the expert on your life.

Task 11. Do a Reality Check.

Looking at your list of chosen goals, make a brief note of your answers to the following questions in relation to each of them:

- What have you done so far towards achieving your goal?

- What more could you do?

- What challenges or difficulties might you encounter?

- How will you overcome them?

- Whose help might you need?

'How do you eat an elephant?

One tiny bite at a time.'

TASK 12 – Make your plan and see it through

It's time now to take each of your goals, break it down into smaller achievable tasks or sub-goals, and assign it a timescale for when you are going to achieve it.

Using a pen and paper (or your computer), set out your plan to look something like the following table.

My Action Plan

GOAL: *It is six months' time, and I am now a stone/6 kilograms lighter and eating a healthier diet. I go to the gym three times per week and swimming at the weekends and when I go on holiday. My clothes fit better. I look and feel great.*

Task	When
Create a healthy menu *(including five portions of fruit and vegetables each day)*	Today
Cut out sweets and junk food	Every day
Use low fat products	Every day
Attend Weight Watchers	Every week
Buy clothes for the gym and pool	Saturday
Complete gym induction	Sunday
Attend gym	Three times per week

Try to keep your plans clear and simple. Focus on taking actions that will help you to achieve your goals. Review and revise your plans regularly (at least once a month) and adjust your timescales as required. When you achieve a goal, celebrate it and reward yourself. You deserve it!

Remember, if you want to change your world you need to think positively and act purposefully.

My Top Tips for Improving Your Life

I wish I could tell you I had some special magical powers to help you on your journey, but that would not be true. Life is not a fairy-tale. I can provide you, however, with some powerful ideas and tools to help unlock your true potential and achieve your desired goals.

- Apply a positive mental attitude to everything you do. Look for the positives in every situation, even (especially) when things go wrong.
- Control your mind-chatter. Replace negative and self-limiting thoughts and beliefs with positive and helpful ones. Become your inner coach, not your inner critic.
- Be careful with your thoughts. They're the blueprints for your actions and emotions. Sow the seeds of the crop you wish to reap.
- Manage your emotions. Learn to recognise and control your emotional responses to people and situations. Negative emotions are usually trying to tell you

that something needs to change. When things go badly wrong, it's OK to feel bad or grieve for a while. But then it's time to move on.

- Let go of the past. Learn from your previous mistakes or misfortunes and think of them not as 'failures', but as opportunities to learn and grow. Failure is your friend.
- Forgive those that may have hurt you. Holding on to anger and resentment only hurts one person. That's *you*.
- Look after your body (it's the only one you'll get). Exercise and enjoy a varied and healthy diet. Take care not to self-medicate too much with harmful substances like food, caffeine, and alcohol and other drugs.
- Imagine and visualise the life you want to live. Visualise the aspects of your life that are working well and the aspects you would like to change. Understand what your priorities are and what's holding you back. (Very often, the answer is YOU.)
- Make a gratitude list. Think about all of the good things in your life and be grateful for them.

- Make a bucket list, too. Write down all the things you would like to do or achieve before you die. Refer to your list and update it often. Encourage others to do the same.

- Set some realistic and achievable goals. Make plans and take purposeful action to achieve them.

- Create positive affirmations, one for each of your goals. Set them in the present tense. Refer to them often and say them out loud.

- Take action! Do something every day that brings you closer to achieving your goals. Use to-do lists or action plans to help you.

- Fill your life with pleasant activities. Try something new. Socialise and reward yourself often. Live your life with passion and purpose.

- Make time in your busy days to relax, meditate, or contemplate. Controlled breathing exercises and candle-lit baths work well. (Wine and soothing music are optional.)

- Connect with nature. Go outside and watch the sun rise, feed the birds, smell the flowers, walk in the park or along the beach, visit the countryside. (Hug a tree if you want to.)

- Do something nice for someone else. Help a friend, family member, neighbour, or stranger. Do voluntary work. Give blood, or give to charity.
- Smile. It's contagious. If you see someone without a smile on their face, give them one of yours. They're free.

Conclusion

I hope you've found this book helpful and insightful and that you'll continue to apply the ideas and techniques to your daily life as you journey on towards greater happiness and fulfilment and the achievement of your goals. I can only point the way, however. The rest is up to you. *Enjoy the journey!*

Clive

P.S. If you would like to attend one of my workshops or hire me as your personal coach, please visit my website www.clivecrossingham.co.uk. (A shameless piece of self-promotion, I know.)

Useful Contacts and Websites (UK)

Mind (mental health information and services)
0300 123 3393   www.mind.org.uk

Rethink (mental health information and services)
0300 5000 927   www.rethink.org

Time to Change (mental health campaign to end stigma
and discrimination)   www.time-to-change.org.uk

Warrington Disability Partnership (disability information
and services)
01925 240064   www.disabilitypartnership.org.uk

Further Reading and Resources

L. Frank Baum, *The Wonderful Wizard of Oz* (George M Hill, 1900).

L. Frank Baum, Michael Patrick Hearn, *The Annotated Wizard of Oz* (W. W. Norton & Co. Inc., 1973).

Martin Davies, *SOD IT!: The Depression 'Virus' and How to Deal with It*, and *SOD IT ALL!: How to deal with the Stress 'Virus' in your Life* (Sod it! Books, 2007).

Paul McGee, *SUMO (Shut Up, Move On): The Straight-Talking Guide to Creating and Enjoying a Brilliant Life* (Capstone, 2006).

Sue Stone, *Love Life, Live Life: How to Have Success and Happiness Beyond Your Wildest Expectations* (Piatkus Books, 2010).

Brian Tracy, *The Brian Tracy Personal Development Seminar Live in the UK* DVD set (National Coaching Academy, 2008).